SOMTOW SUCHARITKUL

rebooting opera for the 21st century

a catalog of Somtow Sucharitkul operatic output
revised 2015

This booklet is a catalogue of Somtow Sucharitkul's operas that are currently available for production, are scheduled to premiere shortly, or are in the planning stages.

Somtow Sucharitkul is one of the tiny number of living composers who specialize in opera and whose operas are regularly produced. He has evolved an extremely accessible yet uncompromising musical idiom that takes into account the history of music in the twentieth century, yet draws as much on the classical and romantic roots of opera and on Asian music and storytelling techniques.

Despite a late start (Somtow's first opera was produced when he was 48) by 2015 a total of eight operatic creations (plus two musicals and ohter stage works) will have reached the stages of three continents. Somtow's operas have not only been praised, but have become more and more popular with audiences; *Mae Naak* was a strong seller in London, and *The Silent Prince* completely sold out its premiere run in Houston. This is perhaps due to Somtow's other career as an award-winning novelist (he has over fifty books in print from major world publishers such as Simon and Schuster and Penguin). His operas tell real stories about people with whom audiences can empathize, and do so using music that is exotic yet easy to grasp. The tropes of twentieth century avant-garde are woven into a largely tonal texture in which melody, rich orchestration and thematic cohesion predominate.

In order to make it easier to see what is available at a glance, and what will become available over the next few years, this catalogue is being made available to the opera-producing world.

Somtow Sucharitkul

OPERAS

already produced and available

MADANA (2001)

The inaugural production of Thailand's Opera Siam (originally Bangkok Opera Foundation) was called "the operatic event of the year" by London's *Opera Now* magazine.'

Based on a play written by King Rama VI, the tale of a king who false in love with a rose who can only become a woman during the light of the full moon translated into a neo-romantic opera in the grand tradition. Of the score, Somtow said, "I eschewed my post-serialist education and for the first time thought about what an audience today might really want to hear." The style that he created for this opera, ("I imagined that Richard Strauss had spent a weekend in Bali") became the basis of an Asian-style "reboot" of the operatic sensibility.

A sumptuous fairy-tale like story, exotic orchestral writing and sweeping, memorable melodies were the main points of attraction of this opera, which also re-energized the career of its composer, who had been semi-retired from music since the late 1970s and had reinvented himself as an award-wining novelist, living in Los

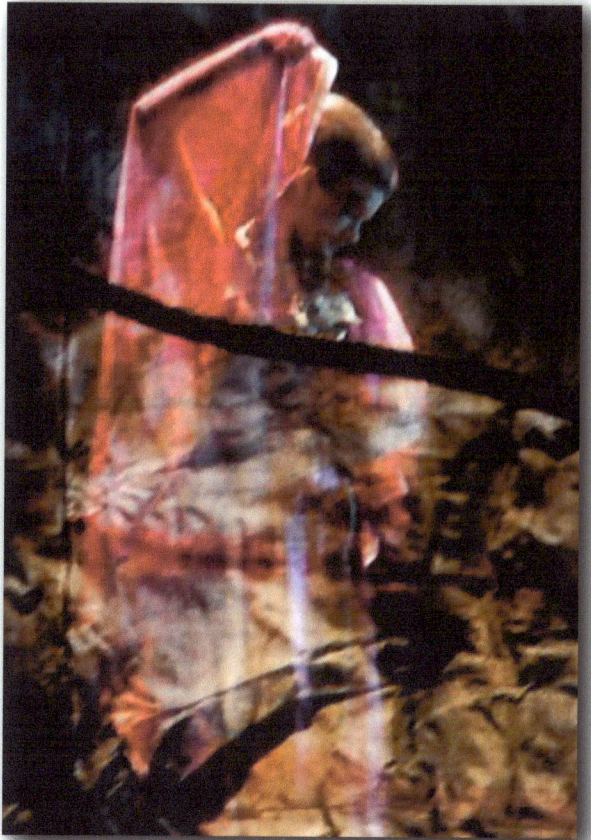

First Production:
February 2001
Bangkok Opera

Cast:
Madana *lyric soprano*
Jayasena *tenor*
Queen Chanti *dramatic soprano*
Arali *mezzo-soprano*
Ascetic *baritone*
Vidura *baritone (may be doubled)*
Sudeva *mezzo-soprano (travesti)*

Chorus
Children's Chorus
Dancers

Orchestration: 2-2-2-2,4-2,3,0, timp,
2 perc, hp, str

Angeles. The success of the production prompted his return to his Asian roots.

The production of *Madana* proved that an opera company could viably exist in Thailand, and as a result, the Bangkok Opera Foundation was created to develop a full opera season. Once this got underway, in only five years Bangkok Opera became in the words of New York's *Opera News,* "the operatic hub of Southeast Asia."

"What Somtow has achieved is not just a marriage between the late-romantic operatic tradition of Richard Strauss with the melodic and philosophical bases of Asian music. He's also broken the barrier between elitism and populism by deliberately forging a new style that blends the Strauss-Mahler-Wagner tradition with accessible melodies and a simple story are that truly mesmerizes its audience. Simply put, this is a break-through not just for the composer, but for Thailand and even for opera itself" — *Thailand Illustrated*

The New York Times

A Thai's Grand Design for Opera

By Brian Mertens
Published: February 24, 2001

The premieres of new operas are fairly rare and often grand occasions around the world, but a recent debut here was an Asian undertaking with little precedent.

A local opera company has never before been assembled in Bangkok. "Madana" was the first opera written by a Thai, the Los Angeles-based composer Somtow Sucharitkul, who is best known as an author of science fiction. It was based on an innovative 1920s play by King Rama VI, who dedicated the drama to one of his wives, Queen Indrasaksachi, a great-aunt of Somtow.

None of this is as unlikely as it seems, Somtow says. "Opera and the arts in general are looking to the East. People run out of new ways to say things, so they start to ransack another culture." "Madana" is just part, he says, of a wave of Oriental influence on Western music.

Somtow attracted many believers — a cast including almost all of Thailand's operatic talent as well as several American singers. He recruited Thailand's top stage director and got sponsors like the Ford Foundation, Mercedes-Benz and the United Nations Educational, Scientific and Cultural Organization. CD and video releases are planned. So is a touring production. Thai high society rose to the occasion, snapping up all the $117 tickets for the gala performance, attended by Princess Galyani Vadhana, the sister of King Bhumibol Adulyadej, and about 70 Somtow fans flew in from the United States. Opera Now magazine called it "one of the operatic events of the year."

Somtow Sucharitkul's new opera MADANA, with a local and international cast and a mostly Thai production team, proved to be an exciting and refreshing experience, full of romantic melodies and textures and a real sense of the theatre. I was not surprised to learn that the composer already has a handful of operas to his credit, although this is the first to be performed in its entirety. There is even a rumour that an early work of this European-educated composer, written in his teens, resides in the archives of the Norwegian Opera in Oslo.

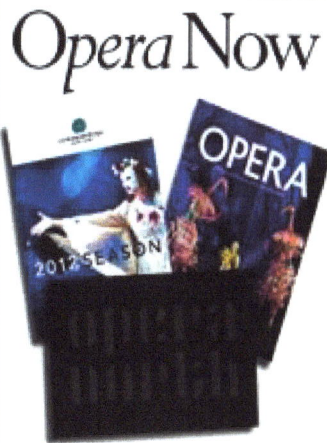

The composer is perhaps better knwn in the West as S.P. Somtow, author of numerous science fiction and horror novels as well as the memoir *Jasmine Nights* (soon to be a film from British production house Radical Media.) As a composer in the 1970s, many of his avant garde wprks were performed in Europe and the US, but he mysteriously vanished from the scene. In this opera, he seems to been reincarnated as a late-romantic composer, successfully combining Asian elements with classically inspired yet original music.

Just how Asian is the music? At first hearing it sounds quite Western, but then you start to hear the concealed elements: the pentatonic opening melody, the constant use of the Balinese *pelog* scale in the accompanying string passages, the ballet music that is based on a haunting Indian raga of the 'mixed' variety. The meat of the opera is completely European -- it is the spices that are Asian, making this a unique operatic experience.

The subject matter of the opera, too, is Asian in the sense that the story is adapted from a play by King Rama VI, but that play is itself inspired in part by Shakespeare.

The story includes all the classic operatic elements: magical transformations, gods, war, betrayal, lust, passion, and revenge. It was all squeezed into a mere two hours of music, along with a children's chorus, an adult chorus, two spectacular ballets, and several intermezzi.

The singing was unformly of a high quality, but special mention should be made of Stacey Tappan's spectacular coloratura technique in the title role. Her attacca top E flat, sustained over a belting orchestra, in her opening aria, was spine-chilling. Her diction is flawless, her voice grand. There is no doubt in my mind that this is an up-and-coming star.

MAE NAAK (2003)

For his second operatic creation for Bangkok Opera, Somtow went to Thailand's most popular ghost story, the tale of *Mae Naak,* the vengeful spirit which has haunted the folk, television and cinematic imagination of Thailand's popular culture for over a century.

The horror motif allowed Somtow to return to his novelistic years as the author of *Vampire Junction* and other bestselling horror novels. Combining *grand guignol* with romanticism and exotic Thai motifs, *Mae Naak* has proved to be Somtow's most popular work so far, which arias such as "Naak's Lullaby" and orchestral

passages such as the opening "Death Dance" frequently being done as concert pieces.

It is Somtow's most frequently revived production and recently completed a three-performance tour in London's *Bloomsbury Theatre,* being the first opera by a Thai to premiere in Europe.

First Production
Bangkok Opera, January 2003
revivals: 2005, 2011,
London 2011

Cast

Naak - *soprano*
Maak - *baritone*
Soldier - *tenor*
Midwife - *mezzo-soprano*
Temple Dancer - *coloratura soprano*
Headman's Daughter - *soprano*
Pork Merchant - *buffo tenor (or baritone)*
Novice - *baritone*
Shaman - *bass*

Chorus and Children's Chorus; Dancers

Orchestration
3d1,2,2,2-4,2,3,0,timp,3 perc, hp, cel, pfte, strings

Opera

The world's leading opera magazine

The Bangkok Opera, which opened its first full season in September 2004, is the kind of company one would usually call a mom-and-pop operation, except in this case there's only a pop. Formed in 2001 by the Thai-born composer and author Somtow Sucharitkul, who has spent a lifetime reconciling his Asian heritage and his Eton-Cambridge education, the company was born of the same cultural tension that has fuelled its founder's art. Somtow, who extended the sonorities and techniques of traditional Thai instruments as a Boulez acolyte in the 1970s, turned to writing genre fiction in the 1980s, when his westernized fantasist's eye gradually rediscovered Thailand's rich folklore. With his latest musical incarnation in the 1990s as a neo-Romantic, those two creative sides have now fused together on the operatic stage.

Mae Naak, Somtow's second opera based on a Thai theme, was billed in the local English-language press as "Thailand's most famous ghost story", though the result on stage was rather more complicated. In brief, the plot concerns a solder going off to war just as he finds out his wife is pregnant; years later, reunited with her, he eventually discovers she is now a ghost haunting others in the village. Out of civic responsibility, he rejects her in this life, hoping to reunite in the next.

While Somtow's libretto bends this traditional tale to modern sensibilities, using flashbacks and other cinematic conventions, his music comes squarely from the opposite direction, stretching a post-Wagnerian Germanic language eastward. The composer's unassuming description in the programme note – essentially, "Thai folk music meets the Hollywood horror movie soundtrack –" was fine for Bangkok's bndding audiences, though more experienced opera listeners could follow a few shrewd brushstrokes of Berg and Bartók.

Little in either the cast or production, however, detracted from the presence of Nancy Yuen, the Hong Kong-born, London-based soprano for whom the title role was written. Though she could deftly negotiate spans of more than an octave in a single phrase, Yuen was often more effective on a single pitch, investing each moment with a range of timbre that communicated on the surface an exquisite emotional depth.

— KEN SMITH

London Fringe Review called it "a stunning work that fuses a European operatic style with Thai folkloric music".

"It deserves to be shown for far more than a short three-night season," the critic wrote. "I recommend that it return to London again."

To celebrate the 60th Regnal Year of King Rama IX of Thailand, Somtow created the opera *Ayodhya*, which is a retelling in a single evening of the complete national epic poem, the *Ramayana*. Using the five-act 'grand opera' structure (with two intervals) Somtow reimagines the story from the point of view of its heroine, Sita.

AYODHYA (2006)

Cast

Sita - *soprano*
Ganesha - *countertenor*
Rama - *tenor*
Ravan - *basso profundo*
Benjakai - *mezzo-soprano*
Lakshman - *baritone*
Hanuman - *baritone*
Lava and Kush - *boy sopranos*

Large chorus; children's chorus

Dancers

Orchestration
3d1, 2, CA, 2, Bcl, 2, Cfg - 6d4, 3, 3, 1 - Timp, 4 perc, 2 Thai perc, 2-4 hp, cel, hpschd, strings

Bangkok Opera may be just six years old, but it has already accomplished more than companies many times its age. Founded by present director Somtow Sucharitkul, it has mounted operas ranging from chamber works like *Dido and Aeneas* and *Turn of the Screw* to full-blown productions of *Madama Butterfly* and *Turandot*. Among other ventures, it has embarked on a Ring cycle *(Das Rheingold* was presented last February; *Die Walküre* is due in July), the first to be fully staged and produced by an Asian company. Bangkok Opera is the only company in southeast Asia operating with a full season (five productions per year). Last November it gave its third world premiere – three performances of *Ayodhya* (seen November 16, 18 & 19) by Somtow, who is both Thailand's leading classical composer and its first to write a western-style opera (*Ayodhya* is his third).

Somtow (surnames are rarely used in Thailand) – composer, conductor, opera director, painter, designer, film director and author of nearly fifty works of horror fiction and fantasy literature - was educated at Eton and Cambridge. He then spent twenty years in Los Angeles, giving him equal familiarity with western culture as with that of his native Thailand. Hence, he is in a virtually unique position of being able to weave Thai motifs and sensibilities into his productions for Bangkok Opera. A recent *Magic Flute* had the Three Boys riding not in an airborne balloon but in a tuk-tuk, and his inspiration for *Das Rheingold* derived more from Buddhism than from Norse sagas.

Somtow composed *Ayodhya* as a personal tribute to the King of Thailand on the occasion of his sixtieth year on the throne. The dedication is doubly appropriate inasmuch as the present king traces his ancestry back to Thailand's first Rama king, the very subject of the opera. Somtow himself is descended from the Rama line, being the great-nephew of Queen Indrasaksachi, wife of King Rama VI who reigned from 1910-1925.

In *Ayodhya*, billed as "a Ramayana for the twenty-first century," Somtow has attempted to compress the famed Indian epic into about two and a half hours of music with two intermissions. Rama and Sita are lovers, but she is abducted by the evil Ravan. The lovers endure long separation, many trials and a bitter war before they are reunited. Yet their renewed relationship is tainted with doubt. "Only the turning of the wheel of the cosmos can heal their love," explains Somtow, putting an eastern twist on an essentially Homeric tale. Audience members who know their Ramayana are at a distinct advantage over those who don't, as the plot unfolds episodically and there are gaps in the English-language libretto's story line.

Yet this defect, one common to many other operas as well, pales beside the grandeur of Somtow's achievement. "I wanted to open up the world of the Ramayana to a new generation of young people who know nothing of Thailand's venerable past," explains Somtow. Despite inevitable technical mishaps associated with a new production, *Ayodhya* remains in this writer's memory as a work greater than the sum of its parts, a feast for both the eye and the ear, a throwback to the era of grand operas that featured stirring choruses, theatrical effects, lavish costumes, big voices, sumptuous orchestration, lyrical melodies and an aura of magic.

The principals came from eight countries. American bass John Ames impressed with his deep, ultra-low voice (down to A below the staff) as the demon Ravan, Russian soprano Marina Zyatkova gave a spectacular display of coloratura as the Golden Deer, England's male alto Michael Chance gave a mesmerizing account of the god Ganesha, and Thailand's own Saran Susebsantiwongse displayed an international class baritone as the monkey god Hanuman.

Director Hans Niewenhuis from Netherlands Opera Studio exploited the wide stage of the Thailand Cultural Center to impressive effect, moving the large cast about in imaginative ways while retaining fluidity of motion. He used state-of-the-art multi-media technology, some of it presumably for the first time in Thailand. His signature technique was a scrim upon which images were projected as visual leitmotifs, helping explain the characters' inner conflicts and lending an element of fantasy to the production. Unfortunately, the scrim also obscured much of what was happening behind it, despite a sophisticated lighting design.

Like the literary source upon which it is based, *Ayodhya* is conceived on an epic scale. The vocal range, spread among eight principals, spans nearly five octaves. The enormous orchestra includes triple-woodwinds, virtuoso writing for piccolo trumpet, a quartet of Wagner tubas, and even a sitar and a harpsichord. Prominent parts for harp and celesta impart a glistening, sparkling sheen to much of the score. Four additional harps and bells are used for the final scene, where Rama and Sita mount the golden stairway to Ayodhya (an eastern variant of Valhalla).

This page: pictures from the world premiere of *The Silent Prince*, Opera Vista, Houston; following pages, from the Bangkok premiere with Opera Siam

Somtow Sucharitkul's *The Silent Prince* is a highly accessible chamber opera designed for easy touring, dramaturgically and musically inspired equally by Western and by South and Southeast Asian models. It is the composer's fourth completed opera.

The Silent Prince is scored for a chamber ensemble of Western and Asian instruments. Easily comprehensible to an opera audience, it nevertheless also partakes of the aesthetics of Asian theatre.

Set in Benares during mythic times, *The Silent Prince* tells the story of a Boddhisatva who must choose between a terrible karmic burden and the dishonor of disobeying his father. To avoid the decision, he withdraws into a world of complete silence, broken only at the end of the story when he appears in the splendor of his divinity to reveal the truth and to redeem his suffering family and people.

The musical language of the opera is an eclectic fusion, inspired equally by the drama and spectacle of baroque opera and the rhythms and colors of Bollywood.

The opera is about 100 minutes long and is in a prologue and five scenes, with a single intermission.

An overprotective mother who thinks her son is God? A virile father who rejects his son's gentle and stereotypical female traits? A deity sent to earth to know great pain and carry the burden of others

Thai composer Somtow Sucharitkul's Bollywood-style chamber opera *The Silent Prince*, although based on an Indian morality tale, crosses many cultural bridges with a comprehensive story line with numerous allegories, tangents and thought-provoking interpretations, all relevant and current.

If you are not familiar with the tales of Temiya, a Buddha reincarnated as a prince who decides to become silent, Sucharitkul's themes are universal and are similar to Judeo-Christian values.

Written in a very comfortable tonal language, Sucharitkul disperses a misconception that contemporary opera is esoteric and impertinent. A world premiere perfect for the Houston stage, the rich and exotic sonorities created by juxtaposing delicious instruments like the traditional Indian tambura with celeste, the church-like harmonium and harp with colorful coloratura flourishes, the effect was mesmerizing capturing an honest, respectful and modern representation of Indian culture.

Sucharitkul's decision to call for a male soprano as Temiya intensified the divine and celestial quality of the moment when *The Silent Prince* is no longer silent. Ryan West was able to capture the moment beautifully with a round tone that floated on top of already shimmering orchestral textures.

"Somtow Sucharitkul's sumptuous and marvellously lyrical score is enchanting," the Houston Chronicle's reviewer wrote, noting the use of traditional Indian instruments in the orchestra - tamburas, celeste and harmonium. He called the show "moving and intriguing" and said it "always retains a deep sense of mystery and spirituality. His rich and beautiful orchestrations are masterful, meaningful and mesmerising."

THE **NATION**
www.nationmultimedia.com

In Somtow Sucharitkul's opera "The Silent Prince", which had its Bangkok premiere at the Thailand Cultural Centre on December 5 in honour of His Majesty the King, Jak Cholvijarn - not just Prince Temiya, the character he played - meditated for almost the entire length of the production. Finally, in the last astonishing five minutes, the Prince revealed himself as a bodhisattva, a man about to become a god.

As in Mozart's operas, where brief silence between notes can speak as eloquently as the music, Jak's enduring quiet made for a transfixing, drawn-out prelude. Temiya withstands incessant distractions and hindrances, then turns to meditate with eyes firmly shut, the better to see the road to becoming the Buddha. Jak, a student of Buddhism, has said that meditating onstage just as surely blocks out distractions so that his soul projects only transcendent good. The power of his silence was riveting.

The show's spirituality was itself a form of meditation, taking audience members to a new understanding of their role in the world. That, Jak explained, was the intention.

Imbued by Wagner, Somtow's newest - and greatest - opera, is composed of the most evocative leitmotifs for violins. It's ethereal, with a seemingly impossible, unworldly beauty, repeatedly drawing the audience to a Buddhist message of goodwill and hope. It's Mozartean in the sense that it operates on many levels, complex sets of themes depicting the battle between good and evil in each of us. "The Silent Prince" is indeed modern-day Mozart: unfathomably profound and yet highly communicative.

Somtow wanted more people to hear about the lives of the Buddha. Temiya was the first of his final 10 reincarnations, a son forced by compassion to disobey his father's command, a sin, to execute a prisoner, also a sin. Temiya retreats into meditation to banish the evil that torments him.

The score was composed with a classicist's clarity, leaving to Trisdee na Patalung and the Siam Philharmonic Orchestra the formidable task of bringing it to life with precision - and without any cloying romance. Trisdee, tolerating my questions while he lay exhausted on a sofa after the performance, acknowledged that the complexity of the music taxed the youthful ensemble pulled into the ranks of world-class musicians.

As Somtow said, the opera has a relatively small cast of 25 performers, but the sound has to be very big. The orchestra's nine strings tackled nine parts in a terrifyingly complex score and the result was quite natural - when not supernatural - leading us into deep reflection. Meanwhile the woodwinds offered intense colour and great beauty and the brass and percussion conjured the forces of Hell with brutish force. It was extraordinary music, played by brilliant musicians!

It is rare when no fault can be found in a production, yet the virtuosity and brilliance in every component of Somtow's tribute to His Majesty allowed for no error.

Nadlada Thamtanakorm as the Queen of Heaven and Goddess of Illusion was simply stunning. Somtow's high notes for her were reminiscent of Mozart's Queen of the Night - and demanding beyond belief. Nadlada had no trouble at all, in a breathtaking display that puts her in the highest class of today's operatic singers. John Ames, in mellifluous bass voice and direct in his enunciation, brought a depth and celestial presence to the King of Heaven, even if his Queen clearly wore the family trousers!

As Sunanda, whom the King of Benares sends to dig a grave for his son (Somtow's libretto here conveyed the macabre genius of his namesake, horror writer SP Somtow), Duo Pan portrayed the compelling power of evil. He was forced to keep digging amid unbearable guilt.

Yet Jak Cholvijarn's performance as Prince Temiya remained the focus of the whole evening. It was extraordinary to watch him sit in meditation, oblivious of swarming seductresses seeking to arouse him and thus prove he was a normal human being. The girls wrapping around the motionless Temiya was hideously sexual, but Jak's frozen features showed that Temiya was no normal human. His rejection of evil was so sublime and powerful that, when Jak finally sang, it was a revelation.

Jak is a true male soprano, his sound pure, without question the voice of an angel from Heaven. As Jak revealed Temiya to be the Buddha, his singing projected one of the finest moments in the history of opera, spirituality made possible through the greatest of music enriching the best that can be found in humanity. It offered hope that we might all embrace the truth of universal love.

As a tribute to His Majesty, on the very day the King exhorted his devoted people to follow the dharma and hold harmony in their hearts, Somtow could not have come up with a better endorsement of the triumphant power of the path to love and truth. "The Silent Prince" is an extraordinary achievement for Thailand, and a gift to the world.

Cast

The King of Heaven - bass
The Queen of Heaven - coloratura soprano
Queen Chanti - mezzo-soprano
King of Kashi - baritone
Amba - soprano
Sunanda - tenor

Orchestra
1 (fl, picc, alt),1 (ob, CA) 1 (Cl, Bcl) 1 - 1,1,1,0, 3 perc, hp, cel, pfte, harm, strings

Chorus
Dancers

SURIYOTHAI (2013)

Somtow Sucharitkul's *Suriyothai* is a ballet-opera based on the story of Thailand's most famous historical heroine. The work became the most successful classical music event in Thailand's history, filling the 2,000 seat Thailand Cultural Center for nine performances, including four extra ones added by audience demand.

Innovatively combining Thai dance styles with the Russian narrative ballet tradition, and then adding snippets of opera, Somtow created a new hybrid art form that showcased the vitality of Siam's cultural life in the 16th Century.

All the main roles are played by dancers except for Queen Suriyothai, cast as both a soprano and a dancer. There is also a large chorus part and a part for a bard who sings in 16th century European style.

Cast

Suriyothai - soprano/dancer
Tabinshvehti - dancer
Mahachakrapt - dancer
French bard - countertenor

Dancers
Chorus

Orchestra
3d1,2,2,2-4,3,3,1-timp, 3 perc,
2 Thai perc., 2 hp, cel, strings

MAHAJANAKA

Mahajanaka is a 45-minute ballet-opera adapted from Somtow Sucharitkul's 1997 *Mahajanaka Symphony,* written in honour the sixth cycle birthday of H.M. The King of Thailand. It is based on the Mahajanaka Jataka, a Buddhist folk-tale which the King himself adapted and modernized for a contemporary audience.

For this staged adaptation, Somtow has added stunning visuals from the paintings of National Artist Chalermchai and the choreography of Puwarate Wongapichat to create a magical new work with chorus, dancers, singers, and a special appearance by Stacey Tappan as the goddess Mekhala.

Mahajanaka is a tale of persistence, endurance, and patience, and about how great things can grow from a single seed. The premiere of this new version celebrates Thailand and the hopes of its people for a brighter future.

World Premiere: July 23, 2014, Thailand Cultural Center
Conductor: Trisdee na Patalung
Director: Somtow Sucharitkul

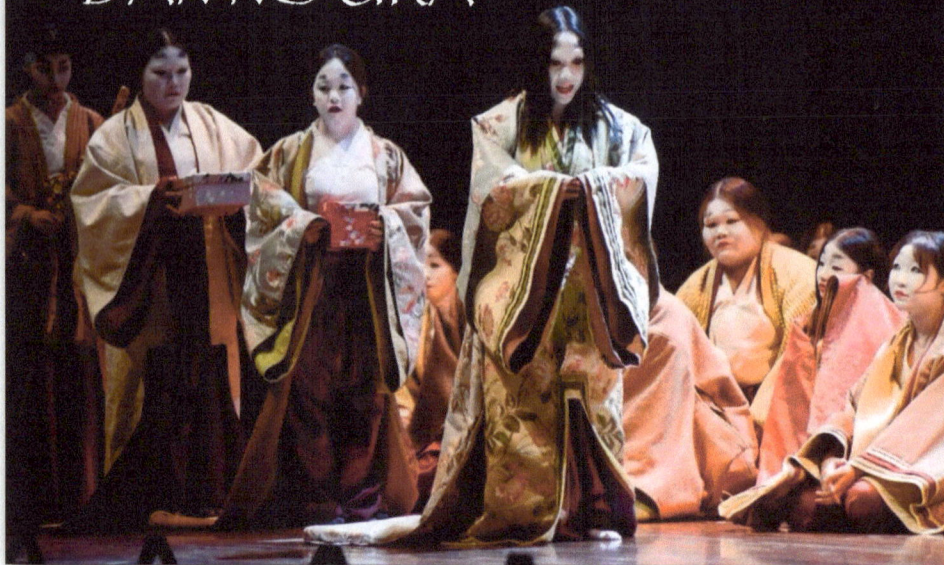

DAN NO URA

In a departure from his last four operas, *Madana, Mae Naak Ayodhya,* and *The Silent Prince,* Somtow Sucharitkul created *Dan no Ura,* an opera about one of the most famous naval battles in history — the Battle of Dan-no-Ura in Twelfth Century Japan. The opera was produced to celebrate the 120th anniversary of Thai-Japanese relations and will premiere at the Thailand Cultural Center at some future date. The opera is inspired by one of Japan's iconic works of literature, *The Take of the Heike,* and Somtow has written the libretto with the help of Alex Kerr, one of the world's most premier Japanologists.

"There is nothing more operatic than the climax of this famous battle," said Somtow, alluding to the celebrated moment in which the nun Nii Dono, grandmother of eight-year-old Emperor Antoku, realizing that all is lost, tells her grandson that she will take him to rule over another capital beneath the sea and, taking the child in her arms, leaps overboard to her death … followed by all the women of the court. For years, since his first encounter with this story in the book *Kwaidan* by Lafcadio Hearn, Somtow has been composing the nun's aria in his head. After learning from officials of TAT that the anniversary was coming up, he accelerated his composing schedule in order to finish the opera within the anniversary year. "I first mentioned this project to the former Japanese Ambassador three years ago," Somtow says. "Everyone agreed that it was amazing that this had not been made into an opera before."

World Premiere: August 11, 2014, Thailand Cultural Center
Conductor: Trisdee na Patalung
Director: Somtow Sucharitkul
Cast: Stacey Tappan, Nancy Yuen, Grace Echauri, Kyu Won Han

The World Premiere performances of Somtow Sucharitkul's "Dan no Ura" in Bangkok on 11th and 12th August confirmed Sucharitkul as one of the most intriguing of contemporary opera composers. Film-like and episodic in construction, it is a continuous two-hour Act of constantly shifting scenes. It is rhythmically complex and demanding for both singers and orchestra, but easily accessible, with many passages of deeply romantic lyricism.

— Auditorium Magazine (Berlin)

A fascinating work, and other companies should be queuing up to stage it.

— Opera Magazine (London)

Somtow's greatest operatic triumph to date.

— Bangkok Post

THE SNOW DRAGON

The Snow Dragon is a chamber opera created to take advantage of more intimate performance spaces with small orchestra pits. The composer has based his libretto on his short 1982 short story *The Fallen Country,* which was original published in the anthology *Elsewhere* from Ace Books. The story was also adapted into a young adult novel by the same name published by Bantam in 1986. The opera centers around the relationship between Dora Marx, a jaded, middle-aged children's counselor who has lost her sense of direction, and Billy Binder, a physically abused young boy whose rage is so powerful it has opened a doorway into another world. But the Fallen Country is not a colorful kingdom of adventure where boys ride dragons and rescue princesses. It is a place of perpetual cold, whose citizens have lost the ability to feel, ruled by the Ringmaster, a sadistic demigod.

Defeating the Ringmaster in the fantasy kingdom is the key to overcoming Billy's problems in the real world, but that is easier said than done. Dora must put aside the comfort zone of her complacency and truly believe Billy's stories, so that she can follow him into the Ringmaster's kingdom … and find redemption for herself as well as the boy. Of the original story, award-winning children's book author Jane Yolen has said: "Somtow manages to combine child abuse and fantasy in such a way as to provide an avenue of healing... "

"In writing this work," the composer says, "I hope to bridge many genres. This work connects opera and fantastic literature, speaks directly to young people in an accessible style which sacrifices none of the subtleties of 'classical opera'. I also aim to create a work on a scale that is easily transportable, in order to bring this world into venues beyond the traditional opera house."

Young people will recognize the the eerie tropes of fantasy and horror film music which make the score very accessible to an audience new to opera. It's also melodically inventive — one of those rare creatures, a modern opera whose tunes can be hummed.

World Premiere: March 14, Skylight Theatre, Milwaukee
conductor: Viswa Subbaraman
director: Matthew Ozawa

BHURIDAT
THE DRAGON LORD

After the success of *Suriyothai,* Somtow created another ballet-opera, this time adapting another of the Buddhist *Jataka* tales, *Buridhat, The Dragon Lord.* In this story, the Bodhisattva comes to earth in the form of a Naga (a sea-dragon) and while deep in meditation is captured by an evil Brahmin and made to perform as a dancing snake in village fairs.

In this work, the non-human nagas are all represented by dancers, while the human characters are performed by opera singers, so that the work literally becomes the intersection of two artistic worlds.

premiere May 22, 2015

Conductor: Trisdee na Patalung
Director: Somtow Sucharitkul

Somtow Sucharitkul

OPERAS

currently in development

HELENA CITRONOVA

Helena Citronova was a Slovak Jew at Auschwitz who had a passionate and searing love affair with Franz Wunsch, an SS-man. For several years, Somtow has been working on an operatic adaptation of this true story.

Somtow writes: "It is based on a true story and one that has stayed with me for many years. It's a story that forces us to ask questions we often dare not ask, like:

- *What is love, in the end? Can love really exist in circumstances like this?*
- *What does being human really mean?*
- *Where is the line that separates our noble aspirations from our hidden darkness?*

"The story has no comfort zones and yet to me it still speaks ultimately of redemption. I wrote the libretto a year ago, and the sound-world I am imagining for the opera is slowly coalescing in my mind."

With the 70th anniversary of the end of the Second World War coming up, Somtow plans to try to finish the opera by 2016.

JOVE IN LOVE

This ballet-opera, planned for 2017, is about the mythological stories behind the four Galilean moons of Jupiter — who represents four of the god's most dramatic love affairs: the story of Io, who was changed into a cow, Europa, for which Jove transformed himself into a bull, the boy Ganymede for whom Jupiter turned into an eagle and carried him off into the sky, and the gender-bending tale of Callisto, whom Jove seduced while disguised as the goddess Diana and who was subsequently changed into a bear.

The four danced stories are narrated from the viewpoint of Galileo, who discovered and named the moons, and who is ultimately responsible — rather than the God — for placing Jove's lovers permanently into the night sky.

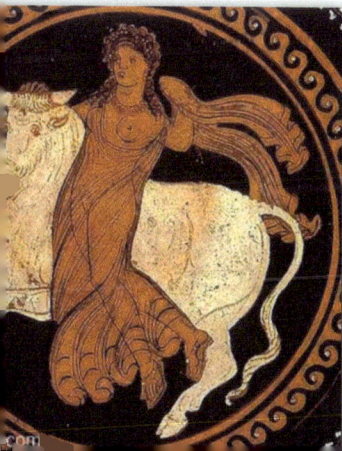

Designed as a picaresque entertainment, the opera interspersed with four mini-ballets will have each ballet designed by a different artist.

The *Dasjati Jatakas* are an epic cycle of the last *Ten Lives of the Buddha*, told and retold all over the Buddhist world for over two thousand years.

Somtow Sucharitkul's opera *The Silent Prince* was premiered in Houston in 2010 to the most stunning reviews ever accorded a work of music theatre by a Thai composer, and the subsequent production created by Opera Siam in 2012 in honour of HM The King of Thailand was the first opera production in Thailand to twice as many ticket applications as available seats.

Building on the spectacular success of his ballet-opera *Suriyothai*, Somtow restructured his *Mahajanaka Symphony*, inspired by another of the Dasjati Jatakas, as a ballet-opera and presented it on the birthday of HRH The Crown Prince of Thailand.

Based on the success of the first two Dasjati Jatakas adapted to music theatre, Somtow has announced that, in honour of the 88th Birthday of HM The King and in tribute to one of the most celebrated royal reigns in history, he will embark on the task of creating music dramas based on all ten of the Dasjati Jatakas.

The task will take five more years to complete and when done, it will entail performance over a five-day festival period. The huge number of characters, the use of different ensembles of Thai and Westerm instruments for each work in the cycle, and the sheer amount of music required to tell the story of ten epic lives will make **Somtow's Das•jati the most ambitious work in the entire history of music and theatre, and the largest integrated work of classical music of all time.**

In 2015, during the birthday celebrations for HRH Princess Sirindhorn, Opera Siam will unveil *Bhuridatta - Prince of Dragons,* and during the King's 88th birthday festivities two more episodes will be unveiled.

The creation of this work is designed to put Thailand permanently on the world cultural map, with festival revivals of the entire cycle to become a fixture of high-

DAS·JATI

The Ten Lives of the Buddha

end tourism, and Asian equivalent to Germany's *Ring Cycle* at the Bayreuth Festival to which audiences come from all over the world and which has a ten-year waiting list.

Educating the world about Buddhism, providing a showcase for the greatest Thai designers, artists and musicians, cooperating with world-class opera stars from all over the globe, and providing a permanent tourist magnet for visitors to spend money in this Thailand, and putting the country squarely in the cultural center of ASEAN are only the beginning of the benefits that will arise when the artists, corporations, and government bodies cooperate to bring this bold vision to life.

Complete Projected Canon for Das-Jati

2010 *The Silent Prince* - premiered by Opera Vista, Houston
2014 *Mahajanaka* - premiered in Bangkok at the International Choir Festival
2015 *Bhuridat* - premiered at the Thailand Cultural Center

Schedule for Remaining works in the Cycle

2015 *Sama The Faithful Son* -
to be premiered at Suryadhep Music Sala
2016 *Nimi Jataka*
2017 *Mahosaddha Jataka*
     Narada Jataka
2018 *Chandrakumar Jataka*
     Vidhura Jataka
2019 *Prince Vessantara*
2020 COMPLETE DASJATI FESTIVAL

Venues to include
Thailand Cultural Center
Suryadhep Music Sala
and others

Once referred to by the *International Herald Tribune* as "the most well-known expatriate Thai in the world," Somtow Sucharitkul is no longer an expatriate, since he has returned to Thailand after five decades of wandering the world. He is best known as an award-winning novelist and a composer of operas.

Born in Bangkok, Somtow grew up in Europe and was educated at Eton and Cambridge. His first career was in music and in the 1970s he acquired a reputation as a revolutionary composer, the first to combine Thai and Western instruments in radical new sonorities. Conditions in the arts in the region at the time proved so traumatic for the young composer that he suffered a major burnout, emigrated to the United States, and reinvented himself as a novelist.

His earliest novels were in the science fiction field but he soon began to cross into other genres. In his 1984 novel *Vampire Junction,* he injected a new literary inventiveness into the horror genre, in the words of Robert Bloch, author of *Psycho,* "skillfully combining the styles of Stephen King, William Burroughs, and the author of the *Revelation to John.*" *Vampire Junction* was voted one of the forty all-time greatest horror books by the Horror Writers' Association, joining established classics like *Frankenstein* and *Dracula.*

In the 1990s Somtow became increasingly identified as a uniquely Asian writer with novels such as the semi-autobiographical *Jasmine Nights*. He won the World Fantasy Award, the highest accolade given in the world of fantastic literature, for his novella *The Bird Catcher*. His fifty-three books have sold about two million copies world-wide.

After becoming a Buddhist monk for a period in 2001, Somtow decided to refocus his attention on the country of his birth, founding Bangkok's first international opera company and returning to music, where he again reinvented himself, this time as a neo-Asian neo-Romantic composer. The Norwegian government commissioned his song cycle *Songs Before Dawn* for the 100th Anniversary of the Nobel Peace Prize, and he composed at the request of the government of Thailand his *Requiem: In Memoriam 9/11* which was dedicated to the victims of the 9/11 tragedy.

According to London's *Opera* magazine, "in just five years, Somtow has made Bangkok into the operatic hub of Southeast Asia." His operas on Thai themes, *Madana, Mae Naak,* and *Ayodhya,* have been well received by international critics. His fourth opera, *The Silent Prince,* was premiered in 2010 in Houston, and a seventh opera, *Dan no Ura,* premiered in Thailand in the August 2014.

In 2015, Skylight Theatre in Milwaukee put on twelve performances of *The Snow Dragon,* an opera based on his short story *The Fallen Country.*

He is increasingly in demand as a conductor specializing in opera. His repertoire runs the entire gamut from Monteverdi to Wagner. His work has been especially lauded for its stylistic authenticity and its lyricism. The orchestra he founded in Bangkok, the Siam Philharmonic, is mounting the first complete Mahler cycle in the region.

In 2013 Somtow was awarded the *Golden W* by the International Wagner Society for his ten years of work in getting Wagner's work promoted and performed in the Southeast Asian region. The youth orchestra he formed, the Siam Sinfonietta, has won First Prize in the Summa cum Laude competition in the Musikverein in Vienna, and in 2014 made its Carnegie Hall debut.

He is the first recipient of Thailand's "Distinguished Silpathorn" award, given for an artist who has made and continues to make a major impact on the region's culture, from Thailand's Ministry of Culture.

www.ingramcontent.com/pod-product-compliance
Lightning Source LLC
Chambersburg PA
CBHW042102040426
42448CB00002B/110